Disclaimer:

This work may not be copied, sold, used as content in any manner or your name put on it without consulting me.

Every effort has been made to be accurate in this publication. The publisher does not assume any responsibility for errors, omissions or contrary interpretation. I do my best to provide the best information on the subject, but just reading it does not guarantee success. You will need to apply every step of the process in order to get the results you are looking for.

This publication is not intended for use as a source of any legal, medical or accounting advice. The information contained in this guide may be subject to laws of South Africa and other jurisdictions. I suggest carefully reading the necessary terms of the services/products used before applying it to any activity which is, or may be, regulated. I do not assume any responsibility for what you choose to do with this information. Use your own judgment.

Any perceived slight of specific people or organizations, and any resemblance to characters living, dead or otherwise, real or fictitious, is purely unintentional.

Some examples of past results are used in this publication; they are intended to be for example purposes only and do not guarantee you will get the same results. Your results may differ from mine. Your results from the use of this information will depend on you, your skills and effort, and other different unpredictable factors.

It is important for you to clearly understand that all marketing activities carry the possibility of loss of investment for testing purposes. Use this information wisely and at your own risk.

Table of Contents

Introduction	04
Section 1: Facebook Remarketing Basics	
Chapter 1: What is Facebook all about	07
Chapter 2: What is Facebook Remarketing?	09
Chapter 3: How can Facebook Remarketing help your business?	12
Chapter 4: Facebook Remarketing Facts to consider	17
Section 2: Facebook Remarketing – Step by Step	
Chapter 5: Facebook Walkthrough	21
Chapter 6: Facebook Ads Manager Walkthrough	25
Chapter 7: Creating a Facebook Remarketing Pixel	29
Chapter 8: Adding the Facebook Remarketing Pixel to your business website	32
Chapter 9: Custom Audiences	35
Chapter 10: Creating a Facebook Remarketing Campaign	38
Section 3: Advanced Facebook Remarketing Strategies	
Chapter 11: Remarketing To Your Existing Customers	45
Chapter 12: Remarketing To App Users	50
Chapter 13: Remarketing To Engagement Audiences	54

Chapter 14: Remarketing To Users Who Never Open Your Emails — 58

Chapter 15: Using Content Series To Remarket To Hard-To-Get Leads — 61

Chapter 16: Additional Facebook Remarketing Tips And Tricks — 65

Section 4: Additional Tips to consider

Chapter 17: Do's and Don'ts — 70

Chapter 18: Premium tools and Services to consider — 75

Chapter 19: Shocking Case Studies — 78

Chapter 20: Frequently Asked Questions — 84

Conclusion — 88

Top Resources — 89

90

Introduction:

Welcome to the latest and very easy to apply "Facebook Remarketing 3.0" Training, designed to take you by the hand and walk you through the process of getting the most out of Facebook, as a remarketing machine for your business.

I'm very excited to have you here, and I know that this will be very helpful for you.

This exclusive training will show you step-by-step, topic by topic, and tool by tool, what you need to know to dominate Facebook Remarketing, in the easiest way possible, using the most effective tools and in the shortest time ever.

This training is comprised of 20 HD training chapters organized into 4 sections. This is exactly what you are going to learn:

Section 1: Facebook Remarketing Basics

In Chapters 1 through 4, we'll talk about:

- ✓ What Is Facebook All About?
- ✓ What Is Facebook Remarketing?
- ✓ How Can Facebook Remarketing Help Your Business?
- ✓ Shocking Facebook Remarketing Facts To Consider

Section 2: Facebook Remarketing – Step by Step

In Chapters 5 through 10, we'll talk about:

- ✓ Facebook Walkthrough
- ✓ Facebook Ads Manager Walkthrough
- ✓ Creating A Facebook Remarketing Pixel
- ✓ Adding The Facebook Remarketing Pixel To Your Business Website
- ✓ Custom Audiences
- ✓ Creating A Facebook Remarketing Campaign

Section 3: Advanced Facebook Remarketing Strategies

In Chapters 11 through 16, we'll talk about:

- ✓ Remarketing To Your Existing Customers
- ✓ Remarketing To App Users
- ✓ Remarketing To Engagement Audiences
- ✓ Remarketing To Users Who Never Open Your Emails
- ✓ Using Content Series To Remarket To Hard-To-Get Leads
- ✓ Additional Facebook Remarketing Tips And Tricks

Section 4: Additional Tips to consider

In Chapters 17 through 20, we'll talk about:

- ✓ Do's and Don'ts
- ✓ Premium tools and Services to consider
- ✓ Shocking Case Studies
- ✓ Frequently Asked Questions

Well, it's time for you to start getting the most out of Facebook as a Remarketing machine, on behalf of your Business.

I know you'll love this training.

Section 1

Chapter 1: What Is Facebook All About

Facebook is a worldwide social media phenomenon. With almost 2 billion active users a month, it has become such a popular platform thanks to its easy to use social platform and features.

The main draw of the Facebook platform is that it allows its users to create personalized social profiles that they can use to get in touch with other users by adding them as friends on their social network.

The platform's popularity along with its accessibility has made it the go-to site to find old friends at a distance and to meet new people. Users can also use Facebook to play games, to chat with their Facebook friends and to share video content.

Facebook users can also create and share photo albums, comment on other people's profiles, and create "groups" where families and groups of friends can share content privately.

Facebook has also become an attractive platform for businesses of all sizes because it offers companies and organizations opportunity across all industries to reach their ideal audience.

Facebook's social nature makes it the perfect online channel for businesses eager to reach and engage potential customers because there they can create their own social profiles in the form of Facebook pages.

Facebook pages are designed to allow small businesses, big companies, brands, organizations, and artists to use the platform the same way that any regular user would, with the added benefit of cost-effectively building a qualified audience.

Furthermore, Facebook Pages allow businesses to promote and remarket their products and services through Facebook's own advertising platform. Tune in to the following chapter to learn more!

Chapter 2: What Is Facebook Remarketing?

Let's now talk about the main topic of this training; Let's talk about a paid advertising strategy so effective that you will wonder why you haven't heard about it before.

Do you think it is unfair to pay top dollar on advertising to reach leads that will click through your ads and then land on your website without taking action, leaving soon after? Do you think that it is unfair that those unconverted leads will possibly forget that they were on your site a few minutes later?

The harsh truth is that the majority of leads that you reach with ads will not convert. In fact, about only 5% of leads end up converting. But what if i tell you that there is a way to re-engage those lost leads, even when they were seemingly uninterested in your business? Let's talk about remarketing and about why Facebook is the perfect remarketing platform.

First, What Is Remarketing?

Remarketing is an online marketing method that advertisers employ in order to stay relevant to bounced traffic and non-converting leads. As a paid advertising strategy it will allow you to reach out to leads long after they have clicked through your ads or visited your website.

Remarketing works by following the steps of your potential customers across the internet. All you have to do is to insert a code provided by your remarketing network on your website that saves a tracking cookie on your visitors' browsers, which then tracks visitors and shows them adverts wherever they go.

The secret behind remarketing's efficiency as an advertising strategy is in how it can help you to reengage leads that have shown an interest in your business not only by clicking on your ads but also by visiting your site while browsing organically.

That is why remarketing is used by many online marketers as a complimentary advertising strategy, as it allows them to send people to the business website that they are promoting through ad units and then to retarget those same users through retargeting ads.

What Makes Facebook The Perfect Remarketing Platform?

As you might already know, Facebook is one of the most effective advertising platforms around, and one that is often preferred by agencies and professional marketers thanks to its cost effectiveness, its wide ad inventory and because of its 2 billion active monthly users.

And it so happens that one of the most lauded features of the Facebook advertising platform is Facebook Remarketing, which offers advertisers better audience targeting options than any other remarketing platform.

That is because the Facebook Remarketing platform allows advertisers to set up custom audiences that go beyond website visitors. With Facebook Remarketing you will be able to retarget existing customers, Facebook app users and in-store customers.

One of the advantages of the Facebook Remarketing platform is that it relies on pixel codes instead of tracking cookies, making up for more accurate remarketing campaigns.

Want to know how else your business can benefit from Facebook Remarketing? Tune in to the following chapter to find out!

Chapter 3: How Can Facebook Remarketing Help Your Business?

If you thought that paid advertising was a necessity, then you will be surprised at how remarketing can help your business, especially on Facebook.

In fact, you would be leaving a lot of money on the table if you don't get into Facebook Remarketing as soon as you finish this training.

Here are the benefits of introducing your business to Facebook Remarketing.

You Will Be Reengaging Potential Customers On The Largest Social Network To Date

Chances are that your potential customers are all already using Facebook. Don't just take our word for it: Studies have found that close to 80% of internet users use Facebook, and a good chunk of them are using it daily, and you can bet that a good portion of your target audience is in that 80%.

That means that, for example, anyone visiting your site is very likely to have Facebook open on another tab on the same browser, which will allow you to immediately show them ads on their newsfeed!

Facebook Remarketing Is Actually Conversion Driven

Most remarketing platforms rely on tracking cookies to retarget website visitors. The bad news is that tracking cookies track all types of visitors, which means that a significant amount of your remarketing budget will go towards retargeting unqualified, uninterested leads.

Facebook on the other hand relies on its marketing pixel code, which actually tracks people who have taken certain actions on your website. These actions can be predefined by yourself, and they include visits to specific pages, items added to shopping carts, time spent on website, and many others.

Facebook Remarketing Increases Brand Recall

Facebook remarketing campaigns are better at generating brand recall than any other remarketing network because they allow your business to connect with potential customers on a more personal level no matter your marketing objective because they will allow you to reach them right when they are using Facebook.

It works because leads that are retargeted with your remarketing ads on Facebook after being on your site will remember your business as the go-to brand when looking for your products or services!

Facebook Remarketing Generates Repeat Business

You can use Facebook Remarketing ads to retarget existing customers in several interesting ways.

For example, you will be able to retarget your customers on Facebook by using data such as their email addresses to offer them upsells and time sensitive offers, which will increase your sales and profits!

Facebook Remarketing Is Cheap

The reason why the majority of small businesses and entrepreneurs decide to not get into paid advertising is not because they are afraid to fail but because they are operating on restricted budgets that do not allow them the luxury to experiment with advertising campaigns.

Facebook advertising though is recognized as a very cheap alternative to most advertising networks, and not cheap in the bad way, but cheap because the platform can afford to allow advertisers to cheaply target its enormous user base.

And it gets better with remarketing, because ads only get cheaper down the pipeline as long as your ad units keep your potential audience engaged.

Want to learn more fascinating stuff about the Facebook remarketing platform? Then make sure to tune in to my following chapter!

Chapter 4: Shocking Facebook Remarketing Facts To Consider

- ✓ While only 2% of website visitors are ready to buy at any given moment, 70% of people that are retargeted through Facebook remarketing campaigns are more likely to convert, which means that business websites are given several second chances to convert the remaining 98%!
- ✓ Facebook remarketing has become such a powerful trend setter when it comes to advertising that 88% of surveyed digital marketers said they used Facebook remarketing.
- ✓ Facebook remarketing campaigns are way more effective when compared to other advertising strategies, generating up to 10 times better click-through-rates when compared to display and search ads.

- ✓ Facebook remarketing can easily improve the performance of other marketing channels. In fact, it has been found that Facebook remarketing can boost search performance by 74%, email marketing performance by 68% and display advertising performance by 61%.
- ✓ Branded searches, or searches generated by brand recall, increase by a whopping 1,046% when inspired by Facebook remarketing, which means that by the simple action of reminding people of your brand's existence with remarketing ads on Facebook you will be increasing the chances of your brand being searched by a thousand times!
- ✓ On the same note, online stores that use Facebook Remarketing tactics to retarget both their potential and existing customers improve their performance by an awesome 726%.
- ✓ On average, as much as 80% of a business' revenue will be generated from only 20% of its existing customer base. But when businesses introduce Facebook Remarketing strategies into their advertising efforts they start seeing a significant

increase in traffic and sales generated by remarketing, with $10 delivered by every $1 spent on remarketing.

- ✓ Facebook has been recognized as the top performing advertising channel by up to 30% of digital marketers, and it has also been recognized as a driving factor into making social media the best performing marketing channel for a lot of marketers due to its powerful social remarketing features. The results speak for themselves: Facebook remarketing delivers 1.77 times more impressions, over two times more clicks and 1.42 times more conversions when compared to other advertising channels.

- ✓ Facebook remarketing on mobile gets even more impressive. Recent studies by third-party Facebook remarketing service providers have found that when marketers add mobile-sized ads to their Facebook remarketing campaigns their average performance increased, with 4% more impressions, 29% more clicks and 15% more conversions!

- ✓ The recent years have seen an increase in the number of marketers dedicating a significant amount of their advertising budget to Facebook remarketing, with up to 14% of marketers spending up to 50% of their advertising budget on it, which means that it works so well that the number of marketers dedicating half their advertising budget on it is growing year after year.
- ✓ 67% of online remarketing service providers are using the "FBX" or "Facebook Exchange" platform to buy their remarketing ad inventory, which means that the Facebook Remarketing platform is the perfect remarketing platform!

Section 2

Chapter 5: Facebook Walkthrough

Unless you have been living under an internet rock for the last 10 years, it is statistically a given that you already have a Facebook account and that you know how to use it for basic social networking, but i consider that in order to teach you all about Facebook Remarketing i need to show you the basic structure of your entire Facebook account first.

Let's start from the very beginning, right after you sign in to your Facebook account and land on the home page, from where you will have access to several tabs and buttons that will take you to every feature offered by your Facebook account.

The most notable feature is Facebook's Newsfeed, which is where all updates and posts from friends and pages will be shown to you. This is perhaps the part of Facebook that you are most familiar with, so let's move on from here.

It is here in the Newsfeed where most Facebook Remarketing Ads are served. They are also served on the right-hand column, so you can expect your remarketing adverts to appear on both placements. Now, right on top of the timeline is the "compose post" section, from where you will be able to create your Facebook posts and updates.

Other types of posts that you will be able to set up from this section include "photo or video album" posts. You will also be able to launch live video sessions using the "live video" feature.

Now moving to the upper panel you can access your profile by clicking on the profile tab with your name and your picture. On your profile menu you will be able to use the "profile" button to go your profile, to "add accounts" or to "switch accounts". On your profile you will find your own timeline, an "about" tab to add and modify your personal info, a "friends" tab to manage your contacts, a "photos" tab to manage your pictures and your photo albums, and a "more" tab to discover detailed information about your Facebook likes.

You can also easily change your profile picture by clicking on the "update your profile picture" button under your current profile picture and to add a cover photo by clicking on the "add a cover photo" button.

By clicking on the "home" tab you can go back to Facebook's home page. By clicking on the "find friends" tab you can see your friend requests, your friend recommendations, and to look for Facebook friends using the filtering options available in the "search for friends" section.

The icons in this panel represent your notifications, and from left to right they are "friend requests", "messages", and general "notifications". The question mark icon is a "quick help" shortcut.

Now, by clicking on the drop-down menu icon you will be able to access "your pages", to view your activity log, to set up news feed preferences, to access your account settings and to log out of Facebook.

You will be able to use the "search" bar on top to use Facebook as a search engine. You will have to enter a keyword in the search bar and then to either click on the search button or to click on any of the search bar suggestions based on the keyword that you entered.

Once in the search results page you will be able to refine your search by "posts", "people", "photos", "videos", "shop", "pages", "places", "groups", "apps", "events", and you can filter your results according to criteria that is unique to each type of result.

Now, on the lower right corner you will find the Facebook messenger, which is the platform's chat feature. You can click on it to see your online contacts and to click on them to start a chat.

Let's now look at the menu on the home page's left-hand column. This menu features shortcuts to basically every feature available on Facebook, including "groups", "events", "games", "live video", "pages feed", "saved" posts, "buy and sell groups" and the "explore feed", among many others.

Lastly, under this menu you will find the options to "create" an "ad", a "page", a "group" or an "event", all right from your Facebook home page.

As you can see, Facebook is a powerful platform that will allow you to do more than basic social networking and browser gaming, with powerful features such as search filters and an advertising dashboard, which is from where you will be doing your Remarketing. We are going to take a detailed look at this Facebook advertising dashboard in the following chapter, so make sure to tune in!

Chapter 6: Facebook Ads Manager Walkthrough

Just like i promised, i am going to walk you through the Facebook advertising dashboard in this chapter, so let's continue right where we left on our previous chapter by clicking on the "ad" shortcut link on the "create" section located under the left-hand column menu to go to the Facebook ads manager.

Now you will have to wait for Facebook to prepare your ad account, to connect to your pages, and to finish getting everything ready for you.

You will then land in the Facebook ads manager main dashboard, from where you are going to access all of Facebook's advertising features, including remarketing. One thing that i would like to highlight is that the ads manager is pretty much optimized to make it easier for you to create ads right from the get go.

The main dashboard is organized in a way that will allow you to create an ad right when you feel like it. The first step is outlined above in the "campaign" section, where you can start by choosing to either "create new campaign" or "use existing campaign" by clicking on each corresponding tab.

Right below the campaign selection section you will find the "what's your marketing objective" section, where you will be able to select your advertising objective. On the left hand menu you have an outline of the steps involved in the ad creation process.

From top to bottom these are "campaign", "ad account", "ad set", and "ad". I am going to go through these steps in detail in my remarketing campaign set up chapter, so let's continue checking out the ads manager. Let's proceed by taking a look at the options in the top panel.

From right to left the first thing you will find is a "help" tab, which you can click to get a condensed help summary with tips about using your Facebook ads manager. Right next to it is the "settings" tab, and clicking on it will take you to the "settings" section.

In the "settings" section you will be able to configure your "ad account setup" from the "ad accounts" tab. Your account setup includes your "ad account id", which can't be changed, your "ad account name", your "time zone" and your "currency" configurations. Your "advertising purpose" can be either set as "yes, I am buying ads for business purposes" or as "no, I am not buying ads for business purposes" depending on how you are operating.

Lastly, you will be able to configure your "business address", "business country" and "tax id number". Now, in the "ad agency" menu you will need to specify whether you are an agency buying ads on behalf of an advertiser or not. In this tab you will also be able to configure your account's "attribution" and to add "ad account roles" if more people besides you are managing this ad manager account.

Now on the "pages" tab you will be able to check and manage your Facebook pages. On the "payment settings" tab you will be able to see your current bills, to "add a payment method", and to "set up your account spending limit", which is a useful feature in case that you are on a tight budget, and you will need to set your limit amount in the "account spending limit" box and then to click on "set limit".

Finally, in the "notifications" tab you will be able to activate or deactivate "all ad account notifications", to specify which "ad email notifications" you want to receive and what type of ad notifications you would like to receive directly on Facebook.

Back on the top panel you will find two notification icons. The first one to the right is the "pages" notification icon, and the next one is the general "notifications" icon. Now, the account icon with your profile picture will allow you to switch between ad accounts in case that you are managing more than one, to log out of your ad account and to go back to your newsfeed.

You will be able to use the "search" bar to find information and help topics about your ads manager, your Facebook ads account as well as your own set ups such as campaigns by entering a keyword or set of keywords.

Now by clicking on the hamburger menu tab to the left you can access the rest of the ads manager features. Section shortcuts in this menu include "plan", "create and manage", "measure and report", "assets", and "settings".

Finally, you can click on the Facebook icon to the far left to go back to Facebook's home page, which is a helpful shortcut once you have finished setting up your campaigns or managing your advertising account. Tune in to my following chapter so i can show you how to create a Facebook Remarketing Pixel from your advertising dashboard!

Chapter 7: Creating A Facebook Remarketing Pixel

I am pretty sure that you are more than eager to start creating your first remarketing campaign on Facebook by now, especially after seeing the ads manager in action, but you won't be able to create the most basic type of remarketing campaign on Facebook unless you create your Facebook pixel first.

Thankfully, this is a pretty easy task to implement, and i am here to guide you through it the right way, step by step. But first things first.

What Is A Facebook Remarketing Pixel?

A Facebook remarketing pixel is simply an HTML element that Facebook uses to track visitors of a website back to

Facebook so it can show them targeted ads on their newsfeeds and on the right-hand column on their home pages. What a Facebook pixel does is to add a tracking code to a specific website page, which in turn reports an action taken by visitors on that specific page back to Facebook, where such visitors are traced and shown ads to.

Have you noticed that when you go to certain websites, such as ecommerce sites, and then go back to Facebook, you start seeing ads promoting products or services offered by those websites on your Facebook home page? That is the Facebook pixel at work. What the pixel did was to track you from the websites that you visited back to Facebook, where ads are shown to you according to the actions that you took on the pages that you visited.

Creating Your Own Facebook Remarketing Pixel

Creating a Facebook Remarketing Pixel is easier than you think, and i am going to show you how right away. First, you have to start by logging in to your Facebook account, and from there go to the ads manager by clicking on the "ad" shortcut link located in the "create" section under the left-hand column menu.

Once in your ads manager dashboard click on the hamburger "tools" menu. Now locate the "measure and report" section and click on the "pixels" shortcut link. You will be taken to the "Facebook Pixels" page. Once there click on the "create a pixel" button. A pop up window will appear with your account's pixel information, and you will have to click on the "create" button to finish.

Awesome! Your new Facebook Remarketing pixel is ready to go. Please note that you will only be allowed to create one Facebook Remarketing pixel per ad account, so you won't have to go through this step after setting it up unless you decide to create additional ad accounts.

Now that you have created your Facebook Remarketing Pixel you can start using it on your website to track your visitors for remarketing. And in order to use your pixel on your website you have to install it there first, and i am going to show you how in my following chapter, so make sure to tune in!

Chapter 8: Adding The Facebook Remarketing Pixel To Your Business Website

Let's continue setting up all the necessary stuff so you can start creating remarketing campaigns like a pro. In this chapter you will be learning how to add the Facebook Remarketing Pixel to your business website, which is pretty easy.

To get started you will have to navigate to the hamburger tools menu on your ads manager dashboard, then to click on the "pixels" shortcut link under the "measure and report" section to go to the "Facebook Pixels" page, and then to click on the "set up pixel" button once there.

As you can see, there are three ways to install your Facebook remarketing pixel on your page. You can "use an integration or tag manager" such as the "Google tag manager" and other third party integration platforms. You can "manually insert the code yourself" by copying the pixel code and inserting it on your website, and you can "mail instructions to a developer" that can take care of installing the pixel for you.

Just as promised, i am going to teach you how to add your new Facebook remarketing pixel to your business website on your own. Start by clicking on the "manually install the code yourself" option. Now scroll down until you find your Facebook Pixel code, and then click on it to copy it to your clipboard.

Once you copy your Facebook pixel code go to your website's main dashboard. Now, what you will have to do is to paste your pixel code in the header section of your website, between the "<head>" and "</head>" tags, as per Facebook's instructions. To do that you have to access your site's header code.

In this chapter i am going to use my own WordPress website to show you how to install the code the easiest ways possible. There are two ways to add this pixel code to a WordPress site. The easiest method is by using the "insert headers and footers" plugin.

To use this plugin to add your pixel to your site you will have to hover over the "plugins" tab on your WordPress dashboard, and then to click on the "add new" option. Now type "insert headers and footers" in the "search plugins" search bar.

Locate the plugin in the search results and click on the "install now" button, then click on "activate" once it installs. Now hover over the "settings" tab on the dashboard left-hand menu and click on the "insert headers and footers" option. Now paste your pixel code in the "scripts in header" field and click on "save". Awesome!

The second method is by actually adding it to the header section of your site's code yourself. Hover over the "appearance" tab on the left-hand menu and click on the "editor" option. Now go to the "templates" menu on the right, locate "theme header" and click on it. Now paste your code between the "<head>" and "</head>" tags, and then click on "update file".

Once you add your pixel code by using either method go back to where you left on Facebook and enter your website's URL in the "send test traffic to your pixel" field and click on the "send test traffic" button.

Awesome! Your Facebook pixel is now active on your site, so click on "continue". In the following step you will have to "add your events". This means that you have to specify what types of actions you want your Facebook pixel to track on your site.

The Facebook pixel will allow you to track actions such as purchases, generated leads, registrations, payment info added by customers, items added to a shopping cart or wish list, initiated checkouts, searches and content views.

Once you have selected which actions to track on your site click on "done". And that's it! You will start seeing activity from your pixel once it starts tracking your website visitor's actions on your site, so keep an eye on it!

Chapter 9: Custom Audiences

I am one step closer to teaching you how to set up your first Facebook remarketing campaign, and because remarketing campaigns require you to first find leads whom to remarket to, you will need to learn to set up custom audiences before creating remarketing campaigns.

In this chapter i am going to teach you where to locate your custom audiences in the ads manager and how to create a basic custom audience to retarget the website visitors that you are tracking with your remarketing pixel.

Start on the Facebook ads manager dashboard and click on the tools hamburger menu icon in the top left corner. Now go to the "assets" column in the display menu and click on the "audiences" shortcut link. You will be taken to the "audiences" page, where you will be able to check, create and edit your target audiences.

To manage and create custom audiences you will have to click on the "create audience" drop down menu and then to click on the "custom audience" option. So before i get started, let's quickly discuss what is a custom audience all about. A custom audience is an audience made of people that have an existing connection or relationship to your business.

Such an audience can be made of people that have bought from your online store before, people in your email lists, people who have visited and viewed content on your website, or people who have engaged with your business before in one way or another, and that you can retarget ads to on Facebook.

As you can see here, there are several interesting ways to remarket to people in a custom audience. You can retarget people in a "customer file", which will allow you to target people according to customer or subscriber information saved in a file.

You can retarget "website traffic", which means that you can remarket to people that have visited your website. You can retarget people by "app activity", which are people who have used your Facebook apps. You can retarget people by "offline activity", such as people that have bought from your offline store or that have provided you with a phone number for doing business. Finally, you can retarget people by "engagement", which are people that have interacted with your content on Facebook.

Now i am going to give you an example of how to create a basic custom audience by selecting the "website traffic" remarketing objective to create a list of who have visited our website using our Facebook pixel.

Once you select the "website traffic" objective you have to start by selecting whom to add to your new custom audience based on your retargeting criteria. You can either include people who meet "any" of your retargeting criteria or people who meet "all" your retargeting criteria.

Now you have to select your retargeting criteria. You can retarget "all website visitors" and enter how many days after they have visited your site you will keep retargeting them.

You can retarget "people who have visited specific web pages" on your site to enter a specific URL from your site from where to track your visitors. This will allow you to qualify interested visitors according to content or actions taken by visitors on those pages. Lastly, you can retarget "visitors by time spent" and select a percentile of time spent by visitors on your site.

You can click on "include" to include additional retargeting criteria, or on "exclude" to add criteria that excludes visitors from being retargeted if they take actions on your excluding criteria.

After you finish selecting your retargeting criteria name your custom remarketing audience in the "audience name" field and then click on "create audience", then click on "done".

Awesome! You are now ready to use this new remarketing audience on a new Facebook remarketing campaign. Tune in to the following chapter so i can show you how!

Chapter 10: Creating A Facebook Remarketing Campaign

Finally, you are now ready to launch your first Facebook remarketing campaign. I know that you have been anxiously waiting to get to this chapter, so let's get started now.

Start on your ads manager dashboard. Please note that you will always land on the "campaign" selection screen by default every time that you open your ads manager account, as you can see here, which greatly simplifies the process.

Now, before creating a campaign you will be able to either "create a new campaign" or to "use existing campaign" in case that you already have campaign set ups saved to use. For this example case i am going to show you how to create a remarketing campaign from scratch.

To create a new remarketing campaign you have to start by selecting your marketing objective. Your marketing objective is what you want to see as a result of creating a Facebook remarketing campaign, such as driving more sales from existing website traffic, or getting more leads to your affiliate pages to increase affiliate profits, among others.

Now, the remarketing objective that you will have to select to leverage existing traffic retargeted by your Facebook remarketing pixel is the "conversions" objective. Once you have selected your objective you will have to scroll down and name your new remarketing campaign in the "campaign name" field, then click on the "set up add account" button.

In the next page you will have to specify your account country, your currency, and your time zone if you haven't done so already. Then click on "continue". Now you will be taken to the "ad set" page, where you will need to select the page you will be using to promote your ad, to set up your audience, your ad placements, your budget and your schedule. Here you will have to start by naming your new ad set in the "ad set name" field.

Now, in the "conversions" section you will have three types of conversions to target: "website", "app" and "messenger". Select the "website" conversion and click on the "please select a conversion event" box to show a list of conversion events. Now select the conversion event that you want to optimize your remarketing ads for. This will depend on the conversion event that you selected during your pixel set up.

In the "offer" section you will have the option to set up offers to drive more conversions on your target destination by turning on the "offer" option. You will need to select from which page you will be promoting an offer and to click on "create offer".

You then will be able to enter your "offer title", your "offer details", an "end date" and "end time" for your offer. You will also be able to select whether to let your customers to redeem your offer "online", "in store" or "both".

You will also be able to generate redemption codes for your offer, to specify how many codes you will give away, and to enter your offer terms and conditions. Once you finalize configuring your offer you will have to click on "create". For this example i am going to focus on the remarketing campaign set up, so i am going to set this up as our offer.

Now move to the "audience" section. Here you will have the option to either "create new audience" or "use a saved audience". In this case, you will have to make use of your custom audiences because you are going to create a remarketing campaign, so you will have to click on the "add custom audiences or lookalike audiences" on the "create new" tab and then to select your custom audience from the custom audience list that will appear.

You can click on "exclude" to select custom audiences to exclude from a campaign as well. Additionally, you can further refine whom to retarget to on your custom audience by adjusting the rest of your audience settings.

Start by selecting a location or series of locations in the "locations" section. You can further refine your target location by going to the "locations" menu and selecting whether to target "everyone in this location", "people who live in this location", "people recently in this location" or "people traveling to this location".

In the "age" section you can select a base age and a top age to target. In the "gender" section you can select to either target "men", "women" or "all". And in the "languages" field you can type a specific language that you might want to target.

In the "detailed targeting" section you can "include" or "exclude" people based on "demographics", "interests", and "behaviors". In the "connections" section you can reach out to Facebook users according to the type of connection that they have with your page, such as "people who like your page" or "friends of people who like your page".

If you would like to target this same audience set up in a future remarketing campaign, you can click on the "save audience" button. Now in the "placements" section you can select "automatic placements" or "edit placements".

Selecting "Automatic placements" will serve your ads to all possible types of users on all types of devices across multiple networks which include third party networks. That is why i recommend that you select "edit placements" so you can select your own ad placements.

My recommendation for you is to select "all devices" and to deselect the "audience network" as well as the "messenger" as placements.

Now in the "budget and schedule" section you have to set up your budget format, amount and schedule. You can either select a "daily budget" if you want to spend a specific amount on a daily basis, or you can select "lifetime budget" if you want to spread a specific amount of money across your campaign's lifetime.

In the "schedule" section you can select the "run my ad set continuously starting today" option to run your ad until you decide to stop it, or you can select the "set a start date and an end date" option to schedule how long to run your new ad set.

My recommendation here is to set a "daily budget" of $5 up $30 if you can afford it, and then start increasing your daily amount until you find a sweet spot where you get good return on investment relative to your remarketing objective.

Now, when it comes to scheduling a remarketing campaign for the first time the best approach is to test it out for 14 to 30 days. You can select "run my ad set continuously starting today" in the "schedule" section to test out your remarketing campaign for a period of time and then stop it manually, or you can select "set a start and end date" and use the calendar option to schedule specific start and end times.

Once you are done here click on "continue". In the following section you will have to edit your ad creative. Enter your ad name in the "ad name" box and select your Facebook page in the "identity" section.

Now in the "format" section you will have to select the format of your ad. The "carousel" format allows you to insert 2 or more images and videos on your ad. The "single image" format will allow you to introduce a single image on your ad. The "single video" format will allow you to use a single video on your ad. Finally, you can select the "slideshow" format to create a looping video ad composed with up to 10 images.

For this campaign you are going to select the "single image" format. You are going to scroll down to the "images" section and click on the "browse library" to select an image for your ad. As you can see here, you will be able to select an image from your library, from a collection of stock images or to "upload images" from your computer.

In this case you are going to select the image from your library that best reflects your offer. Once you make your selection click on "done". Now move to the "Links" section. In this section you will insert your URLs, your ad copy, your headline, your ad text and your calls to action.

Start by entering your landing page's URL in the "website URL" field. Now, in the "headline" field you have to enter an attention-grabbing headline for your remarketing ad. In this case, you are going to enter the name of your business. In the "text" field you will have to enter an inviting "call to action" text related to the content or your offers in the placements that you are tracking on your website.

In the "call to action" menu you can select a working call to action button for your remarketing ad from the vast selection of call to action buttons available. In that case, you are going to select the "no button" option.

Finally, in the "news feed link description" you will have to add a very short but inviting description of your site.

You can check the "ad preview" section on the right-hand side to see how your ad is going to look on different placements, such as desktop and mobile feeds. Once you are done here click on the "confirm" button and wait for your remarketing ad to be approved.

And that's it! Join me in the following section so i can teach you some advanced-level Facebook remarketing strategies!

Section 3

Chapter 11: Remarketing To Your Existing Customers

Let's create a remarketing campaign that you can use to reach your existing customers. Start on the Facebook ads manager dashboard and click on the tools hamburger menu icon in the top left corner. Now click on the "audiences" shortcut link in the "assets" section of the tools menu to go to the "audiences" page.

Now click on the "create audience" drop-down menu and then click on the "custom audience" option. Now select the "customer file" option. This option will allow you to use a customer file to match your existing customers that are registered on Facebook, and to create a custom audience from the matches for remarketing.

You will be given three options to create a custom audience from a customer file. First, you will have the option to "add customers from your own file or copy and paste data", to "import from MailChimp" or to add a "customer file with lifetime value".

To create a remarketing campaign to reach your existing customers you will need to use your own customer file, so click on the "add customers from your own file or copy and paste data" option. First, you will be asked to "add a customer list". To do this you can either "add a new file" or "copy and paste" the customer data.

In this chapter i am going show you how to upload a customer data file to create your customer file audience. When selecting this option i recommend you to use the "download file template" button, to open the file template after it downloads and then to edit the data on the template according to your own customer data.

In this case, you can see how i am going to add a single test customer for this custom audience. I start by clearing all the placeholder data in the template that i am not going to edit over. Now, i am only going to use 5 pieces of customer data for my customer file: my customer's email, first and last names, country of residence and gender, so i clear all the attributes that i am not going to use.

I then edit the placeholder information and enter my own, and then save. Once saved, i can click on the "upload file" button to upload my saved file from my computer. Once uploaded i click on "next".

Now make sure that the correct data is marked green, then click on "upload and create". Wait for your file to load and click on "done". Awesome! Now your customer file audience is saved. Let me now show you how to create the remarketing campaign to reach these existing customers. Start by clicking on the "create ad" button located in the left-hand corner.

Now select your remarketing objective on the "campaign" page. For this example i am going to select the "conversions" objective to retarget my existing customer file audience. Once i have selected my objective i will have to scroll down and name my new remarketing campaign in the "campaign name" field, and then to click on the "conversion" shortcut under the "ad set" section in the left-hand menu.

Start by naming your new ad set in the "ad set name" field.

Now, in the "conversions" section select the "website" option and click on the "please select a conversion event" box to select the conversion event that you want to optimize your remarketing campaign for.

Now select whether to activate or not activate an offer on your ad set in the "offer" section and move to the "audience" section. Click on the "add custom audiences or lookalike audiences" box and on the "create new" tab select your customer file audience from the list.

Now, you won't need to adjust additional audience targeting options in the "audience" section in cases where you are using an existing customer file audience because your audience is already very precisely targeted, and your remarketing campaign will only target people in your customer file that are also registered on Facebook or that can be reached on the audience network.

In light of that, you will have to proceed by scrolling down to the "placements" section. Because your target audience is pretty much defined already, my recommendation is to select the "automatic" placements option in order to reach people in your customer file wherever possible.

Now in the "budget and schedule" section you should set a "daily budget" of $5 up $30, and to select the "run my ad set continuously starting today" option in the "schedule" section to run your ad continuously for 14 straight days under your watch, so you can optimize your remarketing campaigns right after according to your results.

Once done here click on "continue". Now you will have to edit your ad creative. Enter your ad name in the "ad name" box and select your Facebook page in the "identity" section.

Now in the "format" section you will have to select the format of your ad. For this example campaign i am not going to select an image for my ad because i am going to allow Facebook to pull a specific image from my landing page, so i scroll down past the "images" section.

Remember that once in the "Links" section you will have to insert your URLs, your ad copy, your headline, your ad text and your calls to action. Starting in the "website URL" field, enter the specific page where you want your retargeted leads to convert.

In this case, i am going to enter the URL of a page where i reviewed an affiliate product in order to get my retargeted leads to convert by following the affiliate links in my review. This is an effective strategy because they are already familiar with my content and affiliate offers.

Once again, i am going to use the "headline" field to enter the name of my business, which will help my retargeted leads to recall my brand. Then In the "text" field you have to enter copy that is descriptive of the contents on your landing page.

In the "call to action" menu you can select the call to action that best fits your offer or destination content. In my case, i am going to select the "learn more" call to action.

Finally, in the "news feed link description" you can add a brief line of copy with niche keywords that can trigger an emotional response from your leads.

I recommend you to check the "ad preview" section on the right-hand side to see how your new remarketing ad will to look on your target placements. Finally, remember to click on the "confirm" button and to wait for your remarketing ad to be approved. You will get your existing customers coming back on a more regular basis to your site this way!

Chapter 12: Remarketing To App Users

Let's now create a remarketing campaign that you can use to reach your Facebook App users. Start on the Facebook ads manager dashboard and click on the tools menu in the top left corner and click on the "audiences" shortcut link in the "assets" section of the tools menu to go to the "audiences" page.

Now click on the "create audience" drop-down menu and then click on the "custom audience" option. Now select the "app activity" option. This option will allow you to create and retarget a list of people who have launched your apps or games on Facebook.

Now it is time to create your new app user custom audience. Start by selecting whom to either include, people who meet "any" of your retargeting criteria or people who meet "all" your retargeting criteria.

Now select the app that you want to retarget users of. After selecting your app you have to select your app user retargeting criteria in the menu below. There are several app user retargeting criteria available.

You can retarget "anyone who opened the app" and select how many days after opening your app should targets remain in this audience. You can retarget "most active users" and then select the top percentile of active users to target, as well as to select how many days after being active users should remain in this audience.

You can retarget "users by purchase amount" and then select the top percentile of users that have spent the most money on your app as targets, as well as how many days after spending money on your app should targets remain in this audience.

Lastly, you can retarget "users by segment" by targeting segments of app users that you can define by actions taken, demographics, devices used and more. Remember that you can click on "include more" to include additional retargeting criteria, or on "exclude" to add criteria that excludes visitors from being retargeted if they meet your excluding criteria.

Now name your new app user audience in the "audience name" box and click on "create audience". You can now start remarketing to your app users by clicking on "create an ad using the audience".

Now select your remarketing objective in the "campaign" page. For this example i am going to select the "traffic" objective. Now name your new remarketing campaign in the "campaign name" field, and then click on the "ad set" section shortcut in the left-hand menu.

Start by naming your new ad set in the "ad set name" field. Now select the "website" option in the "conversion section". Now select whether to activate or not activate an offer in your ad set in the "offer" section and move to the "audience" section. As you can see, our new app user audience is already selected in the "custom audiences" section because i opted to create an ad with this audience after i set it up.

Remember that you can adjust additional audience targeting options in the "audience" section to better refine your target audience. In this case, i am only going to enter the "English" language in the "languages" section to target English speakers among our app users because i am going to send them to my website.

Now in the "placements" section i recommend you to select the "automatic" placements option in order to reach your app users in all placements.

Now in the "budget and schedule" section i recommend you to set a "daily budget" of $5 up $30 and to select the "run my ad set continuously starting today" option in the "schedule" section to run your ad continuously for 14 straight days.

Now click on "continue" and proceed to edit your ad creative. Enter your ad name in the "ad name" box and select whether to create a new ad or to use an existing post. If you decide to create a new ad, you will have to select your format, your ad images or videos, to edit your links, your copy, and your calls to action.

In my example case, i am going to select the "use existing post" option to use one of my posts with clickable URLs already in place to send app users to my website. I will have to select my Facebook page in the "identity" section and then to select my promoted post on the "creative" section.

Remember to check the "ad preview" section to see how your new remarketing ad will look on your target placements, and then to click on the "confirm" button and to wait for your remarketing ad to be approved. And that is it! Your app users will now be reengaged the right way.

Chapter 13: Remarketing To Engagement Audiences

Let's now show you how to remarket to people who have engaged with your business on Facebook. Start on the Facebook ads manager dashboard and click on the tools menu, then click on the "audiences" shortcut link in the "assets" section to go to the "audiences" page.

Now click on the "create audience" drop-down menu and then click on the "custom audience" option. Now select the "engagement" option. This option will allow you to create and retarget a list of people who have engaged with your content on Facebook or on Instagram.

Now, there are several engagement activities that you can target. You can target "video" engagement to create a list of people who have spent time watching your videos on Facebook or Instagram. You can target "lead form" engagement to create a list of people who have opened or completed a form in your lead ads on Facebook or Instagram.

You can target "full screen" engagement to create a list of people who have opened your collection ads or canvas on Facebook. You can target "Facebook page" engagement to create a list of people who have interacted with your Facebook business page.

You can target "Instagram business profile" engagement to create a list of people who have interacted with your Instagram business profile, and you can target "event" engagement to remarket to people who have interacted with your events on Facebook.

The type of engagement that you select will depend entirely on what type of interactions you want to track and target. In this chapter i am going to show you how to remarket to engagement audiences that have interacted with your Facebook pages by selecting the "Facebook page" option.

After selecting this objective, select whom to include in this remarketing audience, either people who meet "any" of your retargeting criteria or people who meet "all" your retargeting criteria. Now select the Facebook page that you want to remarket people on below.

Now it is time to select your retargeting criteria. As you can see, there are extensive retargeting criteria for Facebook page engagement. You can remarket to "everyone who engaged with your page", "anyone who visited your page", "people who engaged with any post or ad", "people who clicked any call-to-action button", "people who sent a message to your page" and to "people who saved your page or any post".

For this example i am going to select the "everyone who engaged with your page" criteria. Remember that you can click on "include" more to add more additional retargeting criteria and on "exclude" to add excluding criteria.

Lastly, enter your new engagement audience name in the "audience name" box and click on "create audience". You can now start remarketing to your new engagement audience by clicking on "create an ad using the audience".

Select your remarketing objective in the "campaign" page. Once again, i am going to select the "traffic" objective to get more people to my website, where they can check my affiliate content. Name your new remarketing campaign in the "campaign name" field after selecting your objective and click on the "ad set" section shortcut in the left-hand menu.

Now name your new ad set in the "ad set name" field. Select the "website" option in the "conversion section". Now select whether to activate or not activate an offer on your ad set in the "offer" section and move to the "audience" section. You'll notice that your engagement audience is already selected in the "custom audiences" section because you already opted to create an ad with this audience after setting it up.

However, you can always adjust additional audience targeting options in the "audience" section to better refine your target audience. In this case, i am only going to click on "edit locations" to target high-spending English speaking locations and to enter the "English" language in the "languages" section to target English speakers.

Now in the "placements" section i recommend you to select the "edit placements" option and to deselect the "audience network" in order to only retarget engaged users where they are most likely to hang out.

Now in the "budget and schedule" section i recommend you to set a "daily budget" of $5 up to $30 and to select the "run my ad set continuously starting today" option in the "schedule" section to run your ad continuously for 30 straight days.

Now click on "continue" and proceed to edit your ad creative. Enter your ad name in the "ad name" box and select whether to create a new ad or to use an existing post. If you decide to create a new ad, you will have to start from scratch by selecting your ad format, your ad images or videos, to edit your links, your copy, and your calls to action.

In my example case, i am going to select the "use existing post" option to use one of my posts with clickable URLs already in place to engaged users on my website. I will have to select my Facebook page on the "identity" section and then to select my promoted post on the "creative" section.

Remember to check the "ad preview" section to see how your new remarketing ad will look on your target placements, and then to click on the "confirm" button and to wait for your remarketing ad to be approved. And that is it! Your engaged users will now be offered a new way to reconnect with your business online!

Chapter 14: Remarketing To Users Who Never Open Your Emails

Let's create a remarketing campaign that you can use to reach subscribers that never open your emails. Now, the curious thing about this strategy is that it will require you to first create a customer list with the email addresses of the people who do not open your emails. To do so you will need to export a customer file from your Email Marketing service.

In this chapter i am going to show you how to use MailChimp to export a customer file with the email addresses of people who don't open your emails. You will have to log in to your Mailchimp account. Then click on the "lists" tab.

Now go to your list of mailing lists and select the one where you would like to get your non-opening contacts from. Then click on the drop-down menu button corresponding to this list and click on "manage contacts".

On the following page click on the "manage contacts" menu and then click on "view contacts". Now click on the "create a segment" tab. Select "all" in the "contacts match" menu, then go to the "conditions" section below. From left to right, start by selecting the "campaign activity" option from the "subscriber data" menu, then select the "did not open" option on the next menu, and then select "all of the last 5 campaigns" option from the "aggregate campaigns" menu.

Now click on the "preview segment" button. On the following page, click on the "export segment" button, and then click on the "export as csv" button corresponding to your exported segment. Now you will have to decompress your new customer file and go to Facebook.

Once on Facebook go to the ads manager dashboard and click on the tools menu icon. Now click on the "audiences" shortcut link in the "assets" section of the tools menu to go to the "audiences" page.

Now click on the "create audience" drop-down menu and

then click on the "custom audience" option. Now select the "customer file" option. This option will allow you to use your newly created customer file to match your non-opening leads with their Facebook accounts.

So click on the "add customers from your own file or copy and paste data" option to get started. You will now be asked to "add a customer list". You can either "add a new file" or "copy and paste" the customer data.

Because you will be using the customer file that you just created on MailChimp you will have to click on the "upload file" button to upload that file from your computer. Once uploaded click on "next".

Now make sure that the "email" identifier is marked green. You can select other identifiers in your customer list to be added in your customer data map, but i recommend against doing so because this might alter your remarketing results.

Once done here click on "upload and create". Wait for your file to load and click on "done". Awesome! Now you will be ready to show your non-opening customers all that they have been missing out on!

Chapter 15: Using Content Series To Remarket To Hard-To-Get

One of the harshest, inevitable facts of doing online marketing is that, on average, only 2% to 5% of leads convert. That means that over 90% of your leads might not convert at all.

And that is the problem right there with cold advertising: you have to be willing to sacrifice a good chunk of your marketing budget on a non-converting 90% in order to reach the qualified 5%.

Hopefully by now you know how to take care of non-converted leads with remarketing, and i am glad to tell you that i am about to teach you an incredibly effective strategy that will boost your Facebook remarketing performance.

This strategy is the creation of content series. Content series are a linear series of content that are distributed as episodic content. Content series work well because they allow you to capture the attention of uninterested leads in incremental steps.

Content series work on any niche and with any type of content, and you will have to pull data from your finished remarketing campaigns to know who to retarget to with a content series.

Getting Started

You have to start by devising a funnel to deliver your content in incremental steps until you are able to deliver a conversion. Normally, these funnels are separated into three stages: attention, consideration, and conversion.

In the "attention" stage you will have to target a non-converting lead with a remarketing ad offering them access to a non-gated piece of long-form content, which you can do with a clickable single-image or single-video Facebook ad. This will capture the attention of your non-converting lead with brand recall.

In the "consideration" stage you will have to retarget a non-converting lead with a second piece of premium content that is divided into two parts. The one that you will give access to in this second stage is the first part of the content.

You can gauge the interest of the non-converting lead in this stage by setting up a conversion event through your remarketing pixel in the page where this content is served to your non-converting leads.

Finally, in the "conversion" stage you can include an opt-in form at the end of the page where the first part of the content is as well as to set up a remarketing ad with an opt-in form to retarget leads that do not convert on that page in order to get this lead to convert.

It will work because this final piece of content is a gated piece of content that the non-converting lead can access by opting in with their email address.

An example of this would be if you had an eBook for sale, and you see that there are people that visit the sales page for that eBook on a very regular basis, yet they don't buy it, and they don't even opt-in to your email list to receive updates for the eBook in question.

What you have to do then is to create a content series that closely mimics the content of the eBook to make non-converting leads to think that you are releasing the material periodically for free, then ask them for their email addresses before they can access the last part of the content series, and then start remarketing to them right to their email addresses.

Release content three times a week, on Tuesdays, on Thursdays or on Fridays. Finally on Saturday, release the final piece of content, but make it half the content that you have already published.

Once leads reach the final part, send them to a landing page where a summary of the remaining content is presented in bullet-list format. Then send them to a whitepaper landing page after they sign up and send them the rest of the content through email once they sign up.

In any case, here is a summary list of the elements worth relying on when setting up a content series the right way:

- ✓ A blog post dedicated to a piece of content related to the product that hard-to-get leads are interested in. This section needs to be delivered on a three-part basis.

- ✓ A landing page where to send them to once the final piece of content is delivered. Remember that this landing page summarizes the final aspects of the content in bullet-list format.

- ✓ A whitepaper landing page to offer them a freebie with the remaining content in exchange for their email address.

Chapter 16: Additional Facebook Remarketing Tips And Tricks

If there is one thing that we have learned throughout the years is to always keep on learning and experimenting.

The only caveat of trying and experimenting is that you have to fail a lot along the way in order to find what works and what doesn't.

The good thing is that you discover lots of high-level tricks that you wouldn't have been able to find anywhere else otherwise. Here are some of the best tips and tricks that have worked for us over the years!

Remarket To Specific Landing Page Visitors

If there is one constant that you see across Facebook remarketing campaigns is that they tend to target website visitors too broadly.

While it is a good thing to set up a remarketing campaign to reach all website visitors, it is also a good practice to remarket to specific visitors on specific pages.

For example, you can create remarketing campaigns to remarket to visitors of your sales pages. Now, it won't be enough to retarget them with ads but to retarget them with highly targeted ads that are relevant to the people visiting a specific sales page.

Remember To Exclude Converters

You have to always be on the lookout for those leads who have already taken an action, such as people that have read a piece of content, people that have clicked through certain affiliate links and people who have purchased certain products.

Once you identify those converters you will have to exclude them from the campaigns where you were originally retargeting them on and to add them to a different campaign with a different objective to drive a different type of conversion from them, which leads us to myr following tip.

Add A Re-Engagement Stage To Your Remarketing Funnel

The beautiful thing about Facebook remarketing is that it doesn't have to end after you have converted leads, however, you will see lots of marketers neglecting leads after they have converted, thinking that they will come back on their own.

The truth is that very rarely will they come back on their own unless they are brand ambassadors or repeat customers. That is why you have to add "re-engagement" as the last stage in your remarketing funnel.

What this means is that you will have to retarget leads with different remarketing campaigns after converting them on a previous campaign!

Always Split Test Your Remarketing Ads

I recommend you to create different variations of the same ad under the same campaign to track how they perform when targeted at the same audiences.

This will allow you to optimize your remarketing ads based on what works best and to drive more conversions from that effort!

Integrate Your Email Marketing Efforts With Your Facebook remarketing Efforts

Email keeps on being one of the most effective online marketing methods, and what better way to leverage its power than by integrating email with Facebook remarketing?

Facebook allows you to import contacts from MailChimp, so you can sign up for a free MailChimp account, set up your mailing lists there and then to use the "customer file" option when creating a custom audience to import your subscribers to a custom audience on Facebook!

Section 4

Chapter 17: Do's and Don'ts

Do's

Track Efficiently

Depending on your content management system platform and your marketing objective, you will leave a lot on the table if you don't set up an efficient tracking system as well as an efficient tracking strategy after you install your tracking pixel on your website. Using plugins to manage custom audiences and setting up individual retargeting pixels for each website that you will be remarketing from are great starting points.

Segment Your Remarketing Audiences

Segmenting audiences into specific landing page visitors, blog readers, and people who have abandoned your shopping carts, to give you a few examples, is a great way to avoid remarketing to everyone the same way.

Exclude Converters

Remember to exclude people that have converted from your campaigns after they have completed the target actions..

Set Up A Remarketing Funnel

You have to set up a remarketing funnel to move your targets from one step of the customer journey to the other by setting up different remarketing campaigns with different objectives. That way you would be moving your customers from awareness, to consideration, to purchase efficiently.

Match Offers With Qualifying Audiences

You have to match the right type of audience with the right type of remarketing offer. For example, you can retarget visitors that have spent some time reading your material with a free eBook, but you shouldn't retarget them with a sale.

Bid Less For Non-Converters

Non-converters are always going to be a valuable asset as long as they keep coming back, but make sure to not overbid on them.

Keep An Eye On Your Ad Frequency

The highest ad frequency on Facebook remarketing campaigns should be kept at 1 to 3 views, up to 10 views maximum, as that is when the click-through costs will increase!

Split Test

Make sure to test out two or more variations of the same adverts, each one with different assets, and then look at the results to see which variation performs better, then keep optimizing it accordingly.

Review Your Placements

Some audiences respond better to remarketing on certain environments and on certain devices, so make sure to check how well your remarketing materials perform on desktop and mobile, as well as whether they perform better on the newsfeed or on the right-hand column.

Limit Your Ad Appearance

Place a cap on your daily budget to avoid showing your ads to the same people the entire day, or else you will risk your targets getting blind to your remarketing efforts!

Don'ts

Don't Sell Past The Sale

There is no use to keep retargeting people that have converted with a sale with the same offer. Instead, move them to a different campaign where you retarget them with an incentive or an upsell.

Don't Target All Visitors The Same

All your website visitors are different. Some will land on your site by accident, some will be repeat readers, some will be simple researchers, and some will be potential customers in need of a little push to make their final purchasing decision, so target them accordingly!

Don't Overestimate Daily Performance

Daily performance is not an indicator of remarketing success, as there are many factors that can contribute to or affect your remarketing efforts, and some leads can take days or weeks before they engage with your remarketing or convert, so make sure to analyze your performance over time instead.

Don't Ignore High Selling Seasons

You have to prepare season-specific remarketing material to retarget people during national festivities, the holidays, and worldwide spending sprees such as "Black Friday".

Don't Be Repetitive

Don't show the exact same adverts to the same people all the time, as this will cause your remarketing to lose value.

Don't Ask For Useless Lead Info

Don't ask for useless personal information such as phone numbers or addresses to your targets in the consideration stage if it doesn't make sense to your offer. For example, only ask for a first name and email address to people whom you are offering a free eBook to.

Don't Stop Your Campaigns To Early

I've seen many marketers stop their campaigns when they don't see a sale on the first day. Keep in mind that, like i said before, most targets can take days, even weeks, before acting on your remarketing, so be persistent!

Don't Rely On External Analytic Tools

Most external analytic tools such as Google Analytics will give you unreliable data about your Facebook Remarketing, so it's ok to always check your metrics using the ads manager.

Don't Retarget Highly Niche Audiences

Highly niche audiences are not likely to respond to remarketing because the people in such audiences are already the only ones looking after the niche offer in question. In fact, Facebook won't allow you to retarget certain audiences when they're too narrow, so take that into consideration.

Don't Overuse Static Ads

It has been found that remarketing campaigns work best when they serve a combination of dynamic ads such as video ads and carousel ads with static, single image ads, so take your time with your ad creatives!

Chapter 18: Premium tools and Services to consider

Adroll

"Adroll" is an advertising platform popular among big names such as "Salesforce". As a third party Facebook Remarketing provider it offers powerful segmentation features and one of the lowest CPMs available in the industry.

Perfect Audience

"Perfect Audience" is a third-party Facebook Remarketing platform that focuses on capitalizing US based ad impressions on Facebook. It offers an excellent self-serving dashboard that will make it easier for you to track clicks, to drive conversions, and to manage multiple users.

Qwaya

"Qwaya" is a Facebook-focused tool that every remarketer should have in its arsenal. One of its most lauded features is it's "A/B testing" capability, which will allow you to test every ad variable imaginable without spending a dime or launching your campaigns to try them out!

Pagemodo

"Pagemodo" is an advertising tool that provides Facebook Remarketers with a wide selection of ad templates, free of royalty images, powerful ad builder capabilities, built-in retargeting, segmentation, analytics and performance tools!

Driftrock

"Driftrock" is a social media automation tool with powerful features for Facebook remarketers that include signal-triggered ads, automated optimizations, and lead response.

AdSpringr

Most remarketers have a difficult time reading and understanding analytic results, which are vital to optimize remarketing campaigns. "AdSpringr" is an advanced advertising tool for Facebook remarketers looking for a solution, providing them with analysis and performance reporting, optimization, high-level targeting, automated client reporting, automated graphical reporting and visual representation of important Facebook remarketing parameters.

Social Ads Tool

"Social Ads Tool" is a great platform for remarketing agencies and freelancing remarketers that service business owners because it truly delivers lead generation success. It offers automatic ad customizations, deep reporting, and conversion tracking, which is one important metric to track on remarketing campaigns.

AdEspresso

If there is one platform that i would recommend to rookie remarketers, "AdEspresso" would be the one. It is a simplified analytics platform specially designed for Facebook advertisers and remarketers, and it is considered to be one of the simplest, more straightforward analytic tools for digital marketers. It offers easy to understand visual analytics, customizable dashboards, and very detailed metrics.

Conversion Giant

"Conversion Giant" is a remarketing agency that specializes in reengaging the average 94% of people that don't convert after visiting a business website. It's a most popular service as of this date is Facebook Remarketing, and the company itself takes care of everything.

Wordstream

"Wordstream" is a web-based social management software that will allow you to simplify and improve your Facebook remarketing workflow through prescriptive alerts that are customized for the Facebook advertising platform.

Chapter 19: Shocking Case Studies

Thrive

"Thrive" is a digital advertising agency from the US with offices in Dallas, Orlando and other US locations.

Objective: The company's objective was to see how high the Facebook Remarketing pixel could increase metrics such as audience, engagement and reach on a client's campaign.

Strategy: The company's strategy was to un-target vague audience criteria such as interests and behaviors, to create "lookalike audiences" that were similar to the client's current customer base and to position the remarketing pixel in key areas around the client's website.

Results: The campaign achieved peak engagement during the first three months of the campaign, and their client's referral traffic increased by 132% in a single month!

Inbound Ascension

"Inbound Ascension" is a digital remarketing agency founded by Daniel Daines-Hutt, an internationally recognized and certified digital marketer and marketing consultant.

Objective: Daniel's objective was to reach qualified leads whom to sell a digital product in the BETA testing stage of development through Facebook remarketing.

Strategy: Daniel set up remarketing campaigns that only targeted very interested leads and he only served remarketing ads on very specific placements. Daniel also only spent from $0.4 to $0.44 per click through as a challenge.

Results: The campaign made back $297 from each targeted lead, which represents a 675% return on investment from such a small amount per lead!

Chubbies

"Chubbies" is an in-store and online retailer that specializes in colorful, retro-inspired swimwear.

Objective: The company's objective was to increase their reach as well as brand recall.

Strategy: The company split up its Facebook remarketing campaigns with different specific placements. One campaign set was targeting the newsfeed, and another campaign was targeting the right-hand column.

Results: Their remarketing campaigns achieved a pretty cool 35.5% return on investment, lowered their average cost-per-action to 72% below average, and increased their average conversions by 4.8 times within 12 hours of campaign launches.

Marketing Jumpleads

"Marketing Jumpleads" is a UK based marketing agency that has helped around 700 businesses in the UK to succeed.

Objective: The marketing agency's objective was to remarket to "lost costumers" of a British spa and wellness business.

Strategy: The agency created a remarketing campaign to target a "customer file" audience where customers who had not booked a service in three months were added. These "lost customers" received a time-restricted remarketing offer to come back to the spa.

Results: On average, there are 10 to 12 "lost customers" coming back to the spa each month thanks to such Facebook remarketing efforts, each one spending from 80 to 100 pounds per booking.

James Grandstaff

"James Grandstaff" is a digital marketing strategist that specializes in Facebook advertising.

Objective: James' objective was to help a client in the horse training niche who wanted to increase profitability from his existing traffic.

Strategy: James created a Facebook remarketing campaign that targeted website visitors who have completed certain actions and offered them different incentives such as coupons for them to come back and use on the client's website.

Results: James' Facebook remarketing campaign reduced the client's ad spend by almost four times, from $196 all the way down to $59, and got two times more conversions as well!

Design Pickle

"Design Pickle" is a cloud-based graphic design company that provides personalized graphic design support services.

Objective: The company wanted to promote their innovative design service through a free trial that allowed its leads to try its service.

Strategy: The company implemented a Facebook remarketing campaign that targeted visitors on the sales page.

Results: Conversions from the sales page accounted for 17 for every 30 customers, with 50% of new customers generated through the remarketing campaign.

Brian Moran

"Brian Moran" is a digital marketer and the creator of "Samcart", an online tool used by entrepreneurs to maximize their sales.

Objective: Brian's objective was to test how effective Facebook remarketing would be to increase sales of his courses and other training products.

Strategy: Brian created a custom audience to remarket to his existing email list, a lookalike version of his existing email list, and a custom audience using Facebook's native advertising features.

Results: Brian was able to earn $14,114 in profits after spending $8,240 on its remarketing campaign!

Veeroll

"Veeroll" is a video advertising company that specializes in auto-generating video ads for Facebook and YouTube.

Objective: Veeroll's objective was to improve their campaign performance, to track referral conversions from Facebook and to generate leads to reach other businesses.

Strategy: Veeroll implemented Facebook's remarketing pixel on its website to retarget visitors with video ads on Facebook.

Results: By implementing Facebook remarketing on its advertising efforts, Veeroll was able to lower its average cost per click, and to generate 122 new sign ups during the first two weeks, which are generating $11,000 in monthly revenue as of now!

Paul Romando

"Paul Romando" is a successful digital marketer that specializes in creating Facebook marketing strategies and devising digital marketing funnels.

Objective: Paul's objective was to create a specific sales funnel for one of his clients which allowed leads to opt-in for content related to a product in order to drive sales.

Strategy: Paul used Facebook ads to create campaigns to reach and nurture leads through relevant lead magnets, and then created custom audiences where he added leads in the funnel and then retargeted them with product ads.

Results: Paul was able to generate a revenue of $163,969 from $5,989 in ad spend for his client.

Myfix Cycles

"Myfix Cycles" is a Canadian online retailer of single speed and fixed gear bikes for city dwellers.

Objective: The company's objective was to improve their advertising performance.

Strategy: The advertising agency working with Myfix Cycles created a series of custom audiences to target past website visitors, people who have added products to a shopping cart in the past 14 days and people who have made a purchase in the past 180 days.

Results: This Facebook remarketing campaign setup generated $15 in revenue from every $1 spent on Facebook remarketing ads!

Chapter 20: Frequently Asked Questions

Can You Start Remarketing On Facebook Right Away?

Facebook remarketing will only work when you already have regular website visitors, leads subscribed to your lists, or existing customers, to name a few. That is why it is called remarketing. Your best bet would be to first concentrate on engaging people and nurturing leads before getting into remarketing.

How Many People Should There Be On A Custom Audience To Increase Delivery?

While the minimum number of matched contacts that you need to target on a custom audience is 20, the effective number of matches to increase delivery is 100 contacts, and even with 100 contacts you will be reaching minimum delivery, so make sure to first reach over 100 people with your marketing efforts before remarketing to them.

What Are Some Of The Fastest Results That You Can See With Facebook Remarketing?

Recovering and reengaging lost audiences, transforming top-of-the-funnel traffic into engagement and actual conversions, remarketing to people who have been on your website and getting sales from it, upselling to people who have made recent purchases and reengaging product advocates are some of the fastest results that we have seen from Facebook remarketing.

Will Facebook Remarketing Work For You If You Don't' Install The Facebook Pixel On Your Website?

Yes! The Facebook pixel is used to retarget people the classic way, which is by tracking them from your website to Facebook and then showing them ads there. However, there are Facebook Remarketing setups that do not rely on the Facebook pixel such as custom audiences created from a customer file, or custom audiences that retarget people who have engaged with your business on Facebook.

Is The Facebook Remarketing Pixel A Cookie?

Although Facebook pixels and cookies serve a similar purpose, they are different. A pixel is an HTML element that is stored on a confirmation page and that tracks conversions on the page, whereas a cookie is a server-based file that generates a unique ID for every user that visits a website in order to identify and track that user on the web. Pixels in general are more precise than cookies, and they do not expire.

What Is The Benefit Of Using Third Party Facebook Remarketing Platforms?

The main benefit would be that third-party Facebook Remarketing platforms can provide you with custom remarketing configurations that will allow you to simplify your Facebook remarketing workflow.

When Is It Wise To Stop Ads On Third Party Remarketing Platforms To Go Back To Facebook?

There are going to be times when third party remarketing platforms will feel limited to you because they have to go through the Facebook Ad Exchange in order to bid for ad placements, and also because they don't have access to all of Facebook ads inventory.

So the wise thing is to use third party remarketing platforms for convenience, and to go directly to Facebook to set up the more complex remarketing campaigns.

Should You Stop Retargeting Website Visitors To Focus On Nurturing Existing Leads?

Only if you are not getting new website visitors, which is unlikely. What you have to do is to exclude website visitors that do not convert after 30 days of visiting your website, or to retarget them with different incentives depending on the pages they spend the most time on and the actions they take on your website.

What Is The Benefit Of Remarketing To Engaged Customers?

The main benefit of remarketing to the people that are already likely to keep acting on your Remarketing ads is to keep a good "relevance score". The "relevance score" is a metric that dictates how relevant your adverts are. The higher your relevance score is, the less that you will pay for your ads, and the most that they will be shown to your target audience.

Engaged customers sooner or later convert into brand loyalists, and they will keep interacting with your ads and your promoted posts, which will keep your relevance score in good standing. So make sure to create custom audiences to retarget your existing customers!

Should You Keep Your Remarketing Campaigns Running Until You Exhaust Your Budget If You Set A Lifetime Budget?

You will know that it is time to stop your remarketing campaigns when you have reached your remarketing goal, as there is no point in keeping your retargeting ads running after that, which is the easiest way to fatigue your audience.

Conclusion:

We're thrilled that you have chosen to take advantage of our Training Guide, and we wish you amazing success.

And in order to take your Facebook Remarketing Efforts even farther, we invite you to get the most out of it by getting access to our Step by Step Video Training.

Thanks so much for the time you have dedicated to learning how to get the most advantages from Facebook Remarketing.

Facebook Remarketing have come to stay in the market forever.

To Your Success,

Top Resources

Videos
https://www.youtube.com/watch?v=PMC-R28Ev6E
https://www.youtube.com/watch?v=HI-Az637jsI

Tools & Services
https://www.facebook.com/business/news/upgraded-ad-tools
http://www.socialadstool.com/

Training Courses
https://www.udemy.com/facebook-ads-course-beginner-to-advanced/
www.youtube.com/embed/zmqtGXN20bE

Blogs
https://blog.tryadhawk.com/facebook-ads/4-of-the-best-facebook-ad-tools/
https://adespresso.com/blog/

Forums
https://www.warriorforum.com/tags/facebook%20ads.html
https://www.blackhatworld.com/tags/facebook-ads/

Affiliate Programs
https://www.jvzoo.com/
http://www.jvshare.com/

Webinars
https://adespresso.com/webinars/
http://www.cpcstrategy.com/2017-q4-facebook-advertising-summit-webinar-recording/

Infographics
https://www.invespcro.com/blog/facebook-advertising-statistics/
http://www.pagemodo.com/blog/your-2017-small-business-guide-to-facebook-ads-infographic/

Case Studies
https://aggregateblog.com/best-facebook-ad-examples/
https://www.facebook.com/business/success/categories/financial-services

Facts
http://www.jeffbullas.com/23-extraordinary-facebook-advertising-facts/
http://www.soravjain.com/facebook-linkedin-stats-facts-2017

www.ingramcontent.com/pod-product-compliance
Lightning Source LLC
Chambersburg PA
CBHW031436210526
45464CB00005B/2231